Horror Sci-Fi & Fantasy MOVIE POSTERS

volume eleven of
the illustrated history of movies through posters

Images from the Hershenson-Allen Archive

Edited by Bruce Hershenson and Richard Allen
Published by Bruce Hershenson
P.O. Box 874, West Plains, MO 65775
Phone: 417 256 9616 Fax 417 257 6948
mail@brucehershenson.com (e-mail)
http://www.emovieposter.com (website)

STILL AVAILABLE!

ORDER DIRECT

FROM THE PUBLISHER OR CHECK YOUR LOCAL BOOKSTORE. . . IF THEY DON'T HAVE THEM IN STOCK, THEY CAN BE SPECIAL ORDERED.

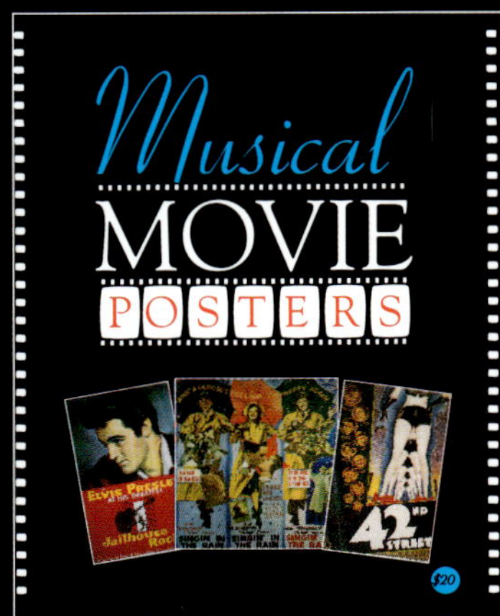

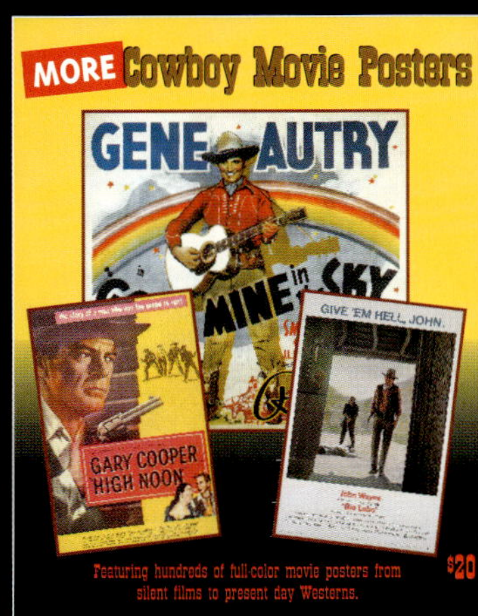

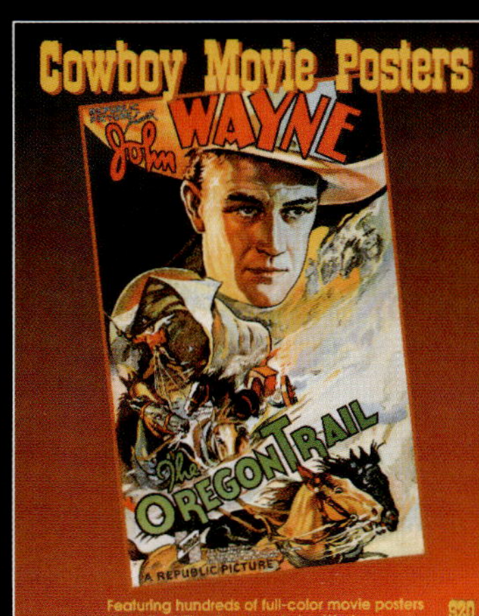

INTRODUCTION

Welcome to the eleventh volume of The Illustrated History of Movies Through Posters. This volume focuses on horror, science fiction and fantasy films. It is a sequel of sorts to volume seven in the series, **Horror Movie Posters**. Because the earlier volume focused solely on the horror genre, this volume has a greater emphasis on fantasy and science fiction. Because the classic films of the 1930s and 1940s were extensively covered in my auction volumes (which are all available as of this writing), this volume focuses more on the years after 1950.

Even so, there were still thousands of images from which I had to choose and I tried to present a cross-section of the genres throughout the history of film, with emphasis on the most important films and the most striking images. There are no duplications from **Horror Movie Posters**, and few duplications from my earlier volumes. The posters are in chronological order to better show the evolution of the genres, with the exception of the Star Wars and Star Trek films, which are grouped together within each series.

All of the images in this book come from the Hershenson-Allen Archive. The archive contains over 25,000 different images of vintage movie posters, covering a high percentage of all the film posters known to exist. Other sources offer some of the same images, but none offer them on high quality 4" x 5" color transparencies, every one of which is photographed directly from the original poster. The Hershenson-Allen Archive was formed in 1997 when Bruce Hershenson, who has sold over thirteen million dollars of vintage movie posters, and published 22 full-color movie poster books, merged his archive with that of Richard Allen, the co-author (with Steve Rebello) of Reel Art, voted one of the hundred greatest books on film. The Archive has furnished hundreds of images for magazines such as Entertainment Weekly, newspapers such as The New York Times, books such as Time-Life Books, and even the U.S. Post Office.

Unless otherwise noted, all of the images in this book are of the standard size movie poster, called a one-sheet and measuring 27" x 41". Other sizes include lobby cards (11" x 14"), half-sheets (22" x 28"), three-sheets (41" x 81"), six-sheets (81" x 81"), and foreign posters (varying sizes).

This series of books represents a quiet revolution in art book publishing. I believe most people would prefer to see more (and larger images) in art books, and will accept a paperback binding and forego the text material if it allows for better printing quality, and more images. Each of the books in this series contain as many images as most coffee table books, yet cost less than half as much and have better printing quality!

This is not a catalog of posters for sale, nor do I sell reproductions!! However I do sell posters of all kinds through sales catalogs and public auctions, so if you are interested in acquiring original vintage movie posters (or the other books I have published), visit my website at http://www.emovieposter.com, or send me a self-addressed stamped envelope for free brochures.

I need to thank Richard Allen, my co-compiler in this book and many previous volumes. He continually tracks down elusive images that greatly enrich this series. I also need to thank Sylvia Hershenson, who proofread this book and prepared the index and cutlines; Amy Regez of Sullivan/Santamaria Design, who did the layout and designed the cover; and the printer Courier Graphics.

I dedicate this book to my long-time friend and frequent business partner, Ron Barlow. In 1972, Ron and I co-published a collection of horror comics by fantasy artist Berni Wrightson, and soon after began publishing the very first reprints of classic EC comics. It was Ron who re-introduced me to the movie poster hobby in the early 1980s, which led to my full-time involvement which has lasted over ten years. Ron has been a great friend for 30 years. I cherish our friendship and thank him for all he has done for me over the years.

Bruce Hershenson
November 1999

1. HOMER'S ODYSSEY, 1909, special poster

2. A TRAP FOR SANTA CLAUS, 1909

3. THE PIED PIPER OF HAMELIN, 1913

4 THE GHOST OF SLUMBER MOUNTAIN, 1918, six-sheet

5. THE CABINET OF DR. CALIGARI, 1921, German promotional poster

6. A CONNECTICUT YANKEE IN KING ARTHUR'S COURT, 1921, 1920s reissue

7. THE HUNCHBACK OF NOTRE DAME, 1923, lobby card

8. STORMSWEPT, 1923

9. THE THIEF OF BAGDAD, 1924, half-sheet

10. DANTE'S INFERNO, 1924, lobby card

11. SHE, 1925, lobby card

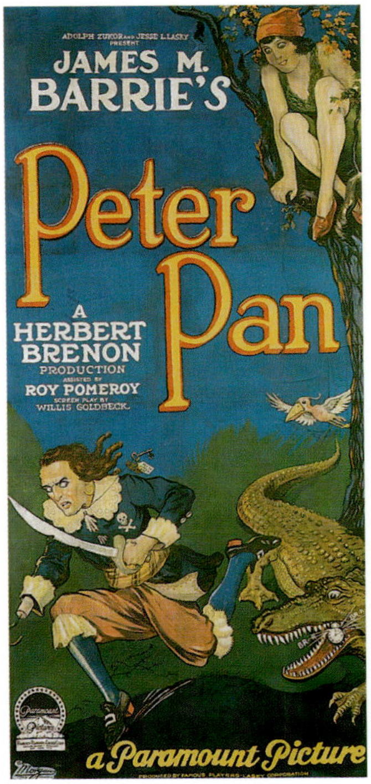

12. PETER PAN, 1924, three-sheet

13. THE WIZARD OF OZ, 1925, Title card

14. THE WIZARD OF OZ, 1925, lobby card

15. THE WIZARD OF OZ, 1925, lobby card

16. THE WIZARD OF OZ, 1925, lobby card

17. MICHAEL STROGOFF, 1926

18. THE WOMAN IN THE MOON, 1929, Swedish poster

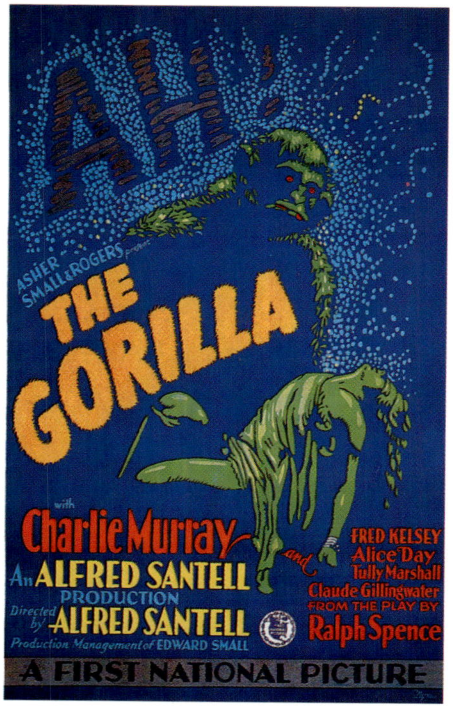

19. THE GORILLA, 1927

20. THE MYSTERIOUS ISLAND, 1929, lobby card

21. DRACULA, 1931, Title card

22. FRANKENSTEIN, 1931, Title card

23. A CONNECTICUT YANKEE, 1931

24. INGAGI, 1931

25. MONSTERS OF THE DEEP, 1931

26. DR. JEKYLL AND MR. HYDE, 1931, Swedish poster

27. CONGORILLA, 1932

28. FREAKS, 1932

29. KING KONG, 1933, six-sheet

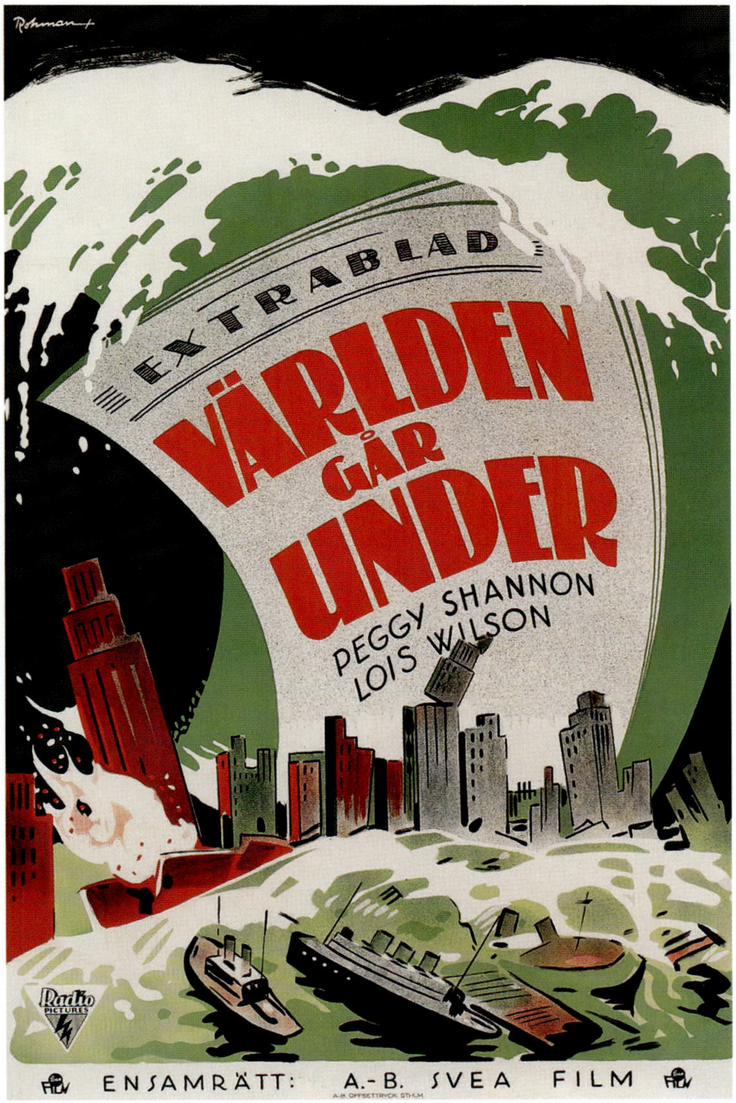

30. DELUGE, 1933, Swedish poster

31. TRANSATLANTIC TUNNEL, 1935

32. DANTE'S INFERNO, 1935

33. THE GHOST GOES WEST, 1935,
undated reissue

34. A MIDSUMMER NIGHT'S DREAM, 1935

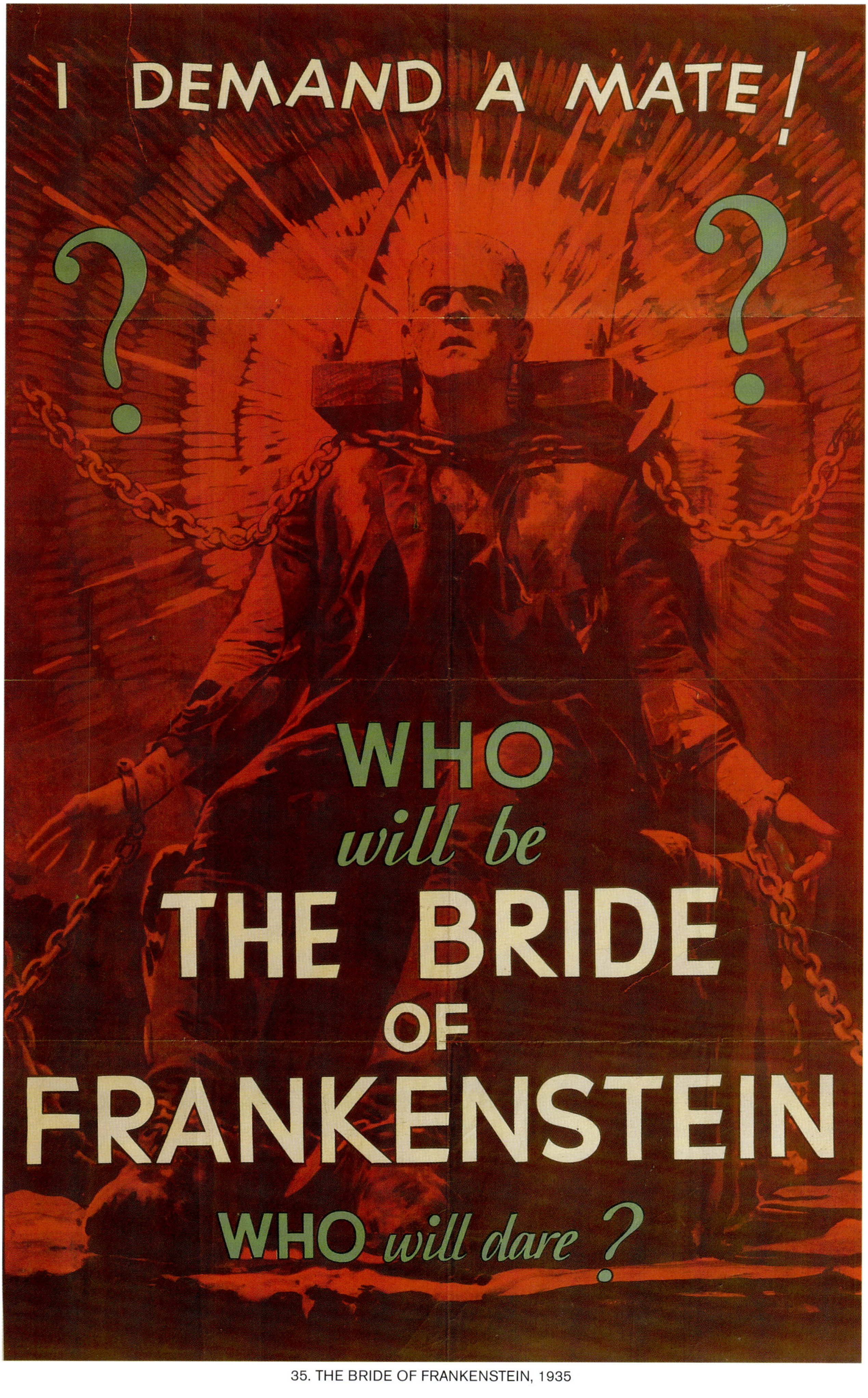

35. THE BRIDE OF FRANKENSTEIN, 1935

36. THE GREEN PASTURES, 1936, lobby card

37. NON-STOP NEW YORK, 1937, half-sheet

38. THINGS TO COME, 1936, six-sheet

39. TOPPER, 1937, Italian poster

40. THE MAN WHO COULD WORK MIRACLES, 1937, Danish poster

41. LOST HORIZON, 1937, three-sheet

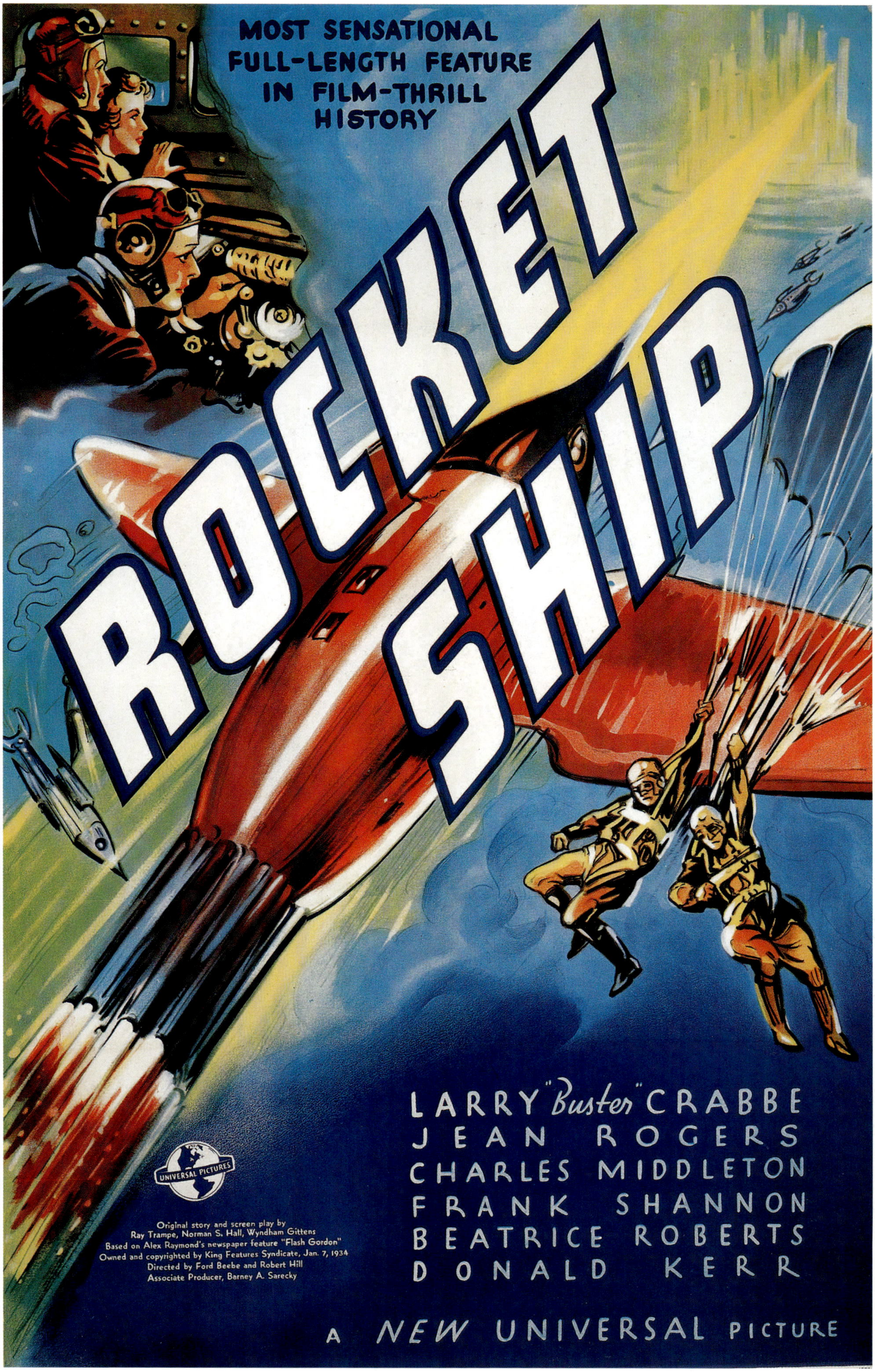

42. ROCKET SHIP (MARS ATTACKS THE WORLD), 1938

43. THE WIZARD OF OZ, 1939

44. THE THIEF OF BAGDAD, 1940, Italian poster

45. THE WOLF MAN, 1941

46. THE GHOST BREAKERS, 1940

47. THE BLUE BIRD, 1940

48. INVISIBLE GHOST, 1941

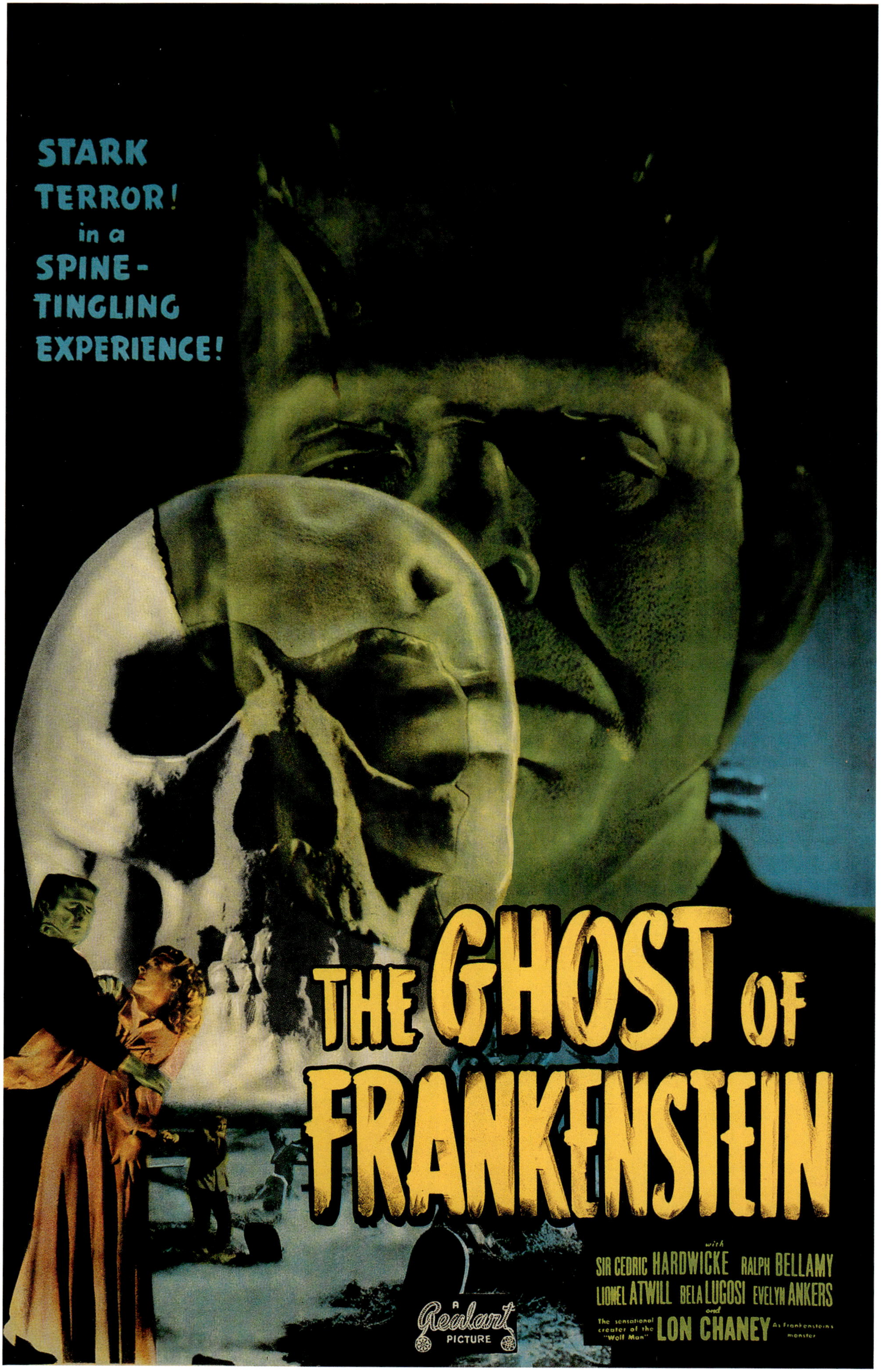

49. THE GHOST OF FRANKENSTEIN, 1942, 1949 reissue

50. RUDYARD KIPLING'S JUNGLE BOOK, 1942

51. CAT PEOPLE, 1942

52. I MARRIED A WITCH, 1942

53. HEAVEN CAN WAIT, 1943

54. THE UNINVITED, 1944

55. THE CANTERVILLE GHOST, 1944

56. THE PICTURE OF DORIAN GRAY, 1945, Australian daybill

57. THE ENCHANTED COTTAGE, 1945

58. THE HORN BLOWS AT MIDNIGHT, 1945

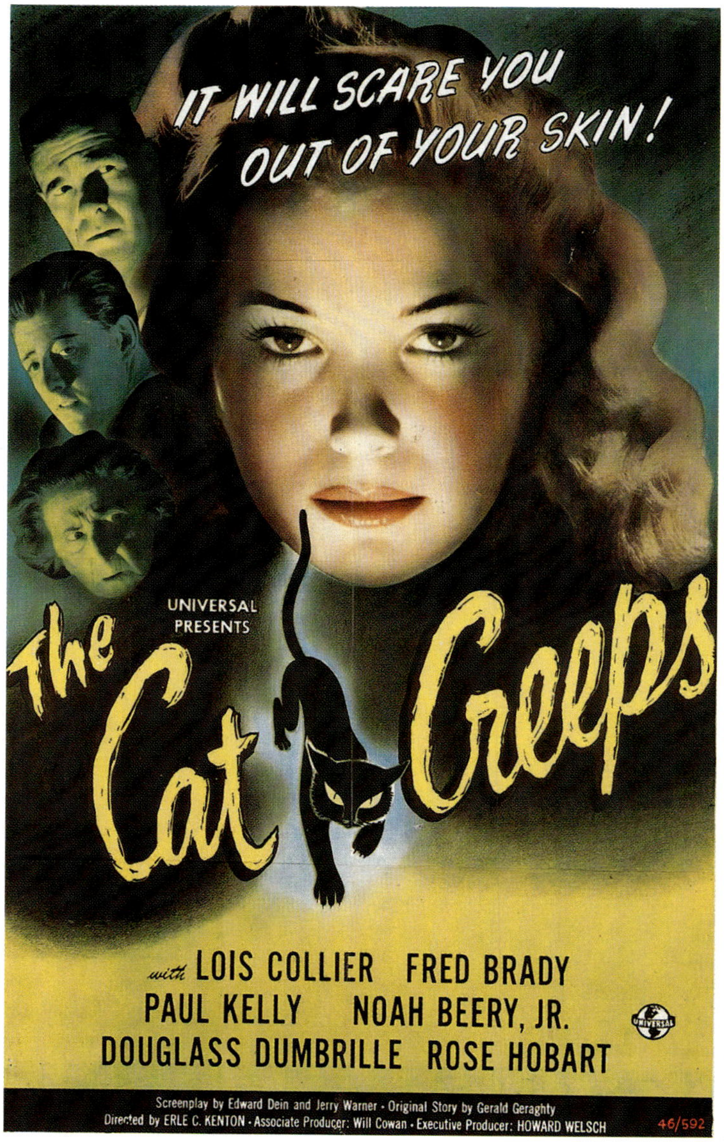

59. THE CAT CREEPS, 1946

60. IT'S A WONDERFUL LIFE, 1946

61. ANGEL ON MY SHOULDER, 1946

62. THE SECRET LIFE OF WALTER MITTY, 1947

63. THE GHOST AND MRS. MUIR, 1947

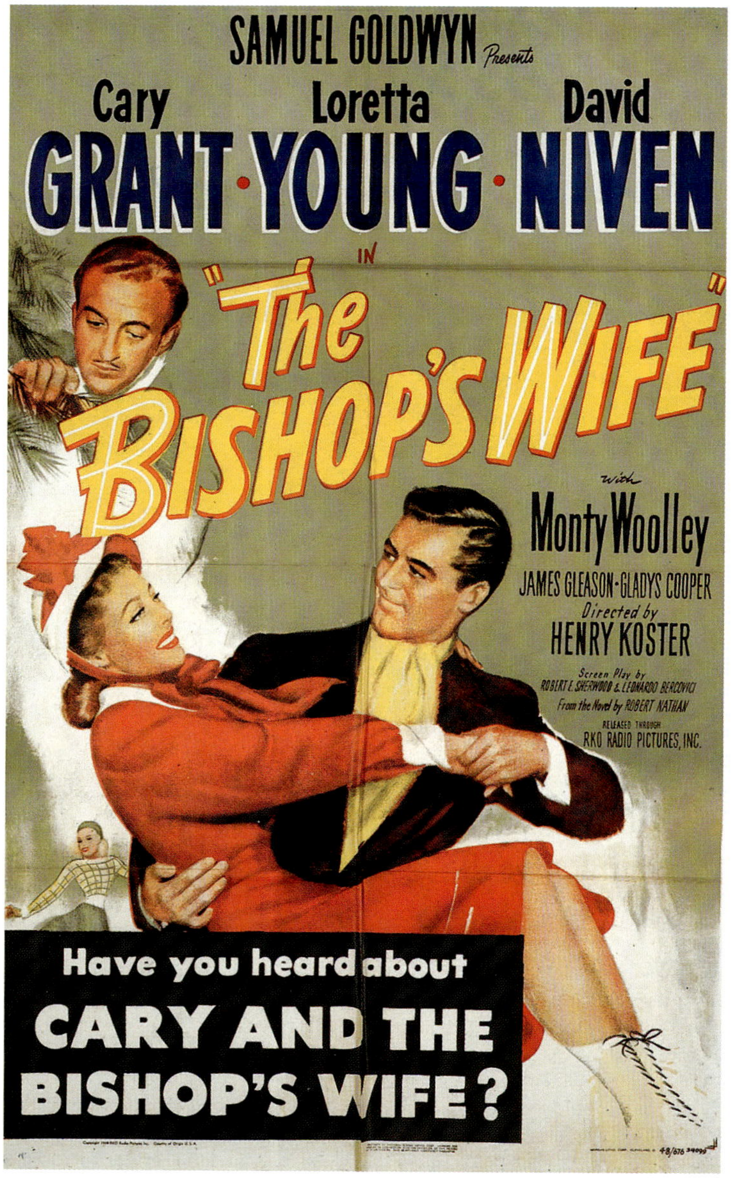

64. THE BISHOP'S WIFE, 1947

65. PORTRAIT OF JENNIE, 1948

66. MIRACLE ON 34TH STREET, 1947

67. MR. PEABODY AND THE MERMAID, 1948

68. ABBOTT AND COSTELLO MEET FRANKENSTEIN, 1948

69. THE BOY WITH GREEN HAIR, 1948

70. MIGHTY JOE YOUNG, 1949

71. A CONNECTICUT YANKEE IN KING ARTHUR'S COURT, 1949

72. HARVEY, 1950

73. KING OF THE ROCKET MEN, 1949

74. DESTINATION MOON, 1950, Italian poster

75. SUPERMAN AND THE MOLE MEN, 1951

76. FLIGHT TO MARS, 1951

77. PANDORA AND THE FLYING DUTCHMAN, 1951

78. THE DAY THE EARTH STOOD STILL, 1951

79. DOCTOR JEKYLL, 1951, Italian poster

80. WHEN WORLDS COLLIDE, 1951, Mexican poster

81. SPACEWAYS, 1953, Italian poster

82. RED PLANET MARS, 1952

83. PHANTOM FROM SPACE, 1953, Italian poster

84. IT CAME FROM OUTER SPACE, 1953, Danish poster

85. MONSTER FROM THE OCEAN FLOOR, 1954, half-sheet

86. THE 5000 FINGERS OF DR. T, 1953

87. INVADERS FROM MARS, 1953, Italian poster

88. TARGET EARTH, 1954

89. THIS ISLAND EARTH, 1954, Forty By Sixty

90. TARANTULA, 1955, half-sheet

91. THE ROCKET MAN, 1954

92. TOBOR THE GREAT, 1954, Italian poster

93. CREATURE FROM THE BLACK LAGOON, 1954, French poster

94. GODZILLA KING OF THE MONSTERS, 1956

95. CREATURE WITH THE ATOM BRAIN, 1955

96. CONQUEST OF SPACE, 1955

97. THE BAD SEED, 1956

98. IT CAME FROM BENEATH THE SEA, 1955, Italian poster

99. ON THE THRESHOLD OF SPACE, 1956, Italian poster

100. FORBIDDEN PLANET, 1956, Forty By Sixty

101. 1984, 1956, Italian poster

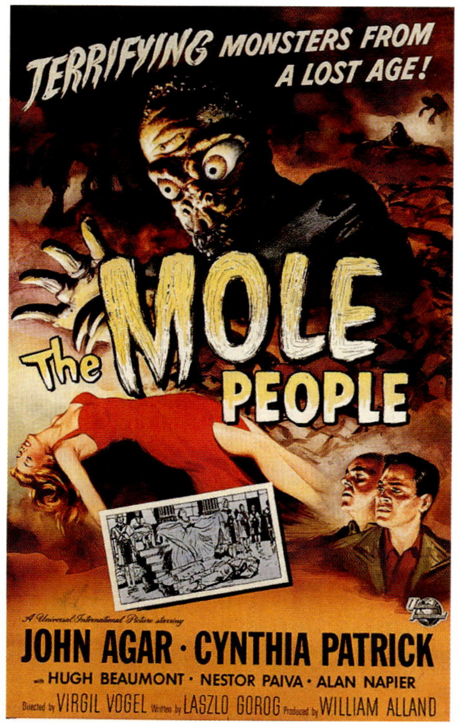

102. THE MOLE PEOPLE, 1956

103. AROUND THE WORLD IN 80 DAYS, 1956

104. FORBIDDEN PLANET, 1956, Italian poster

105. 20 MILLION MILES TO EARTH, 1957, Italian poster

106. THE LAND UNKNOWN, 1957

107. COSMIC MONSTERS, 1957

108. LOVE-SLAVES OF THE AMAZONS, 1957

109. THE MONSTER FROM GREEN HELL, 1957, Italian poster

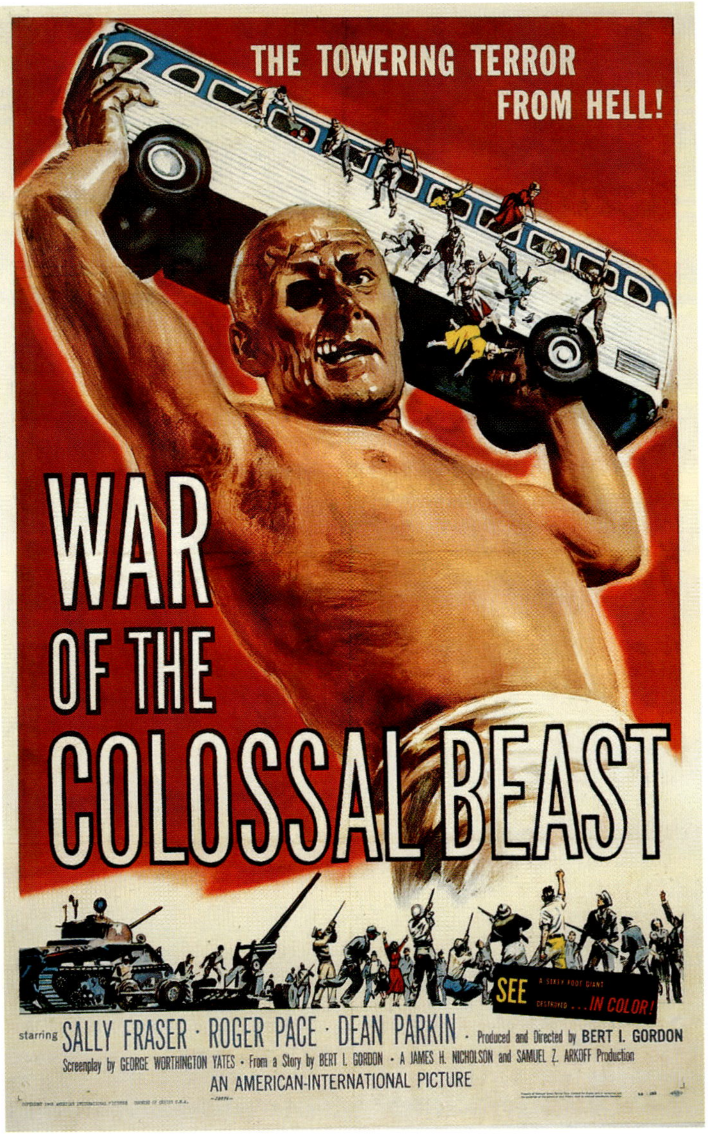

110. WAR OF THE COLOSSAL BEAST, 1958

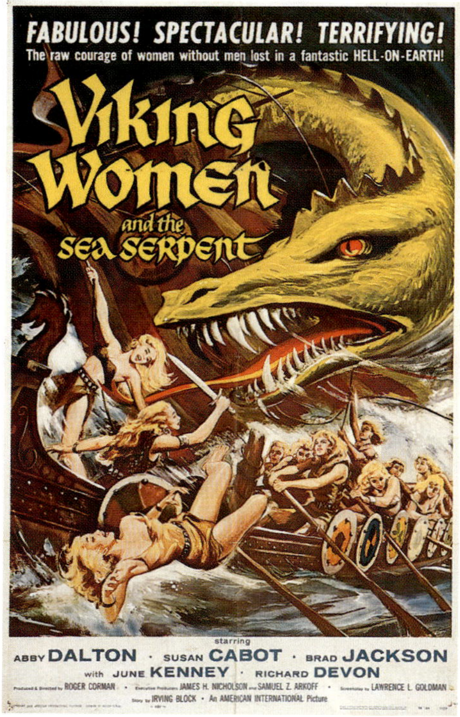

111. VIKING WOMEN AND THE SEA SERPENT, 1958

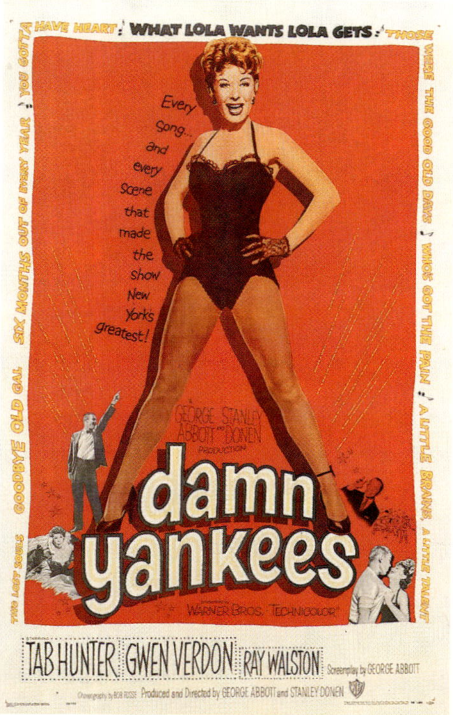

112. DAMN YANKEES, 1958

113. SHE GODS OF SHARK REEF, 1958

114. THE BLOB, 1958

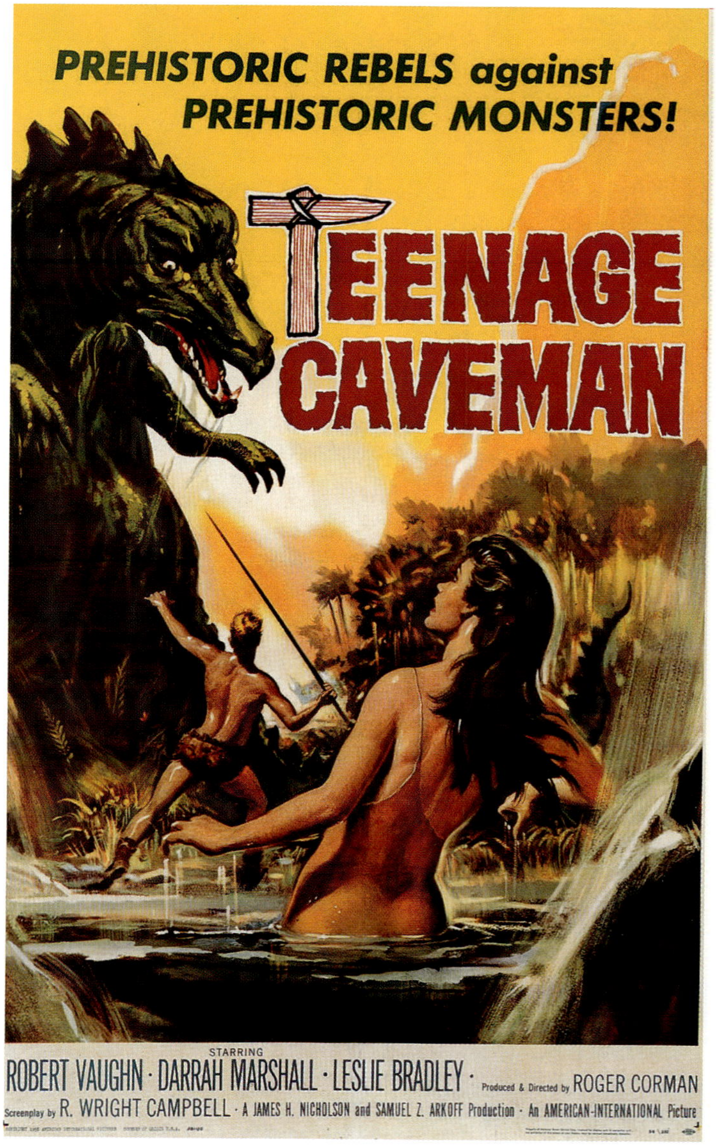

115. TEENAGE CAVEMAN, 1958

116. ATTACK OF THE 50 FT. WOMAN, 1958

117. THE SHAGGY DOG, 1959

118. TEENAGERS FROM OUTER SPACE, 1959

119. THE WORLD, THE FLESH AND THE DEVIL, 1959

120. ON THE BEACH, 1959

121. THE MOUSE THAT ROARED, 1959

122. JOURNEY TO THE CENTER OF THE EARTH, 1959

123. ATTACK OF THE JUNGLE WOMEN, 1959

124. DARBY O'GILL AND THE LITTLE PEOPLE, 1959

125. THE ANGRY RED PLANET, 1959

126. ASSIGNMENT-OUTER SPACE, 1960

127. BATTLE IN OUTER SPACE, 1960

128. 12 TO THE MOON, 1960

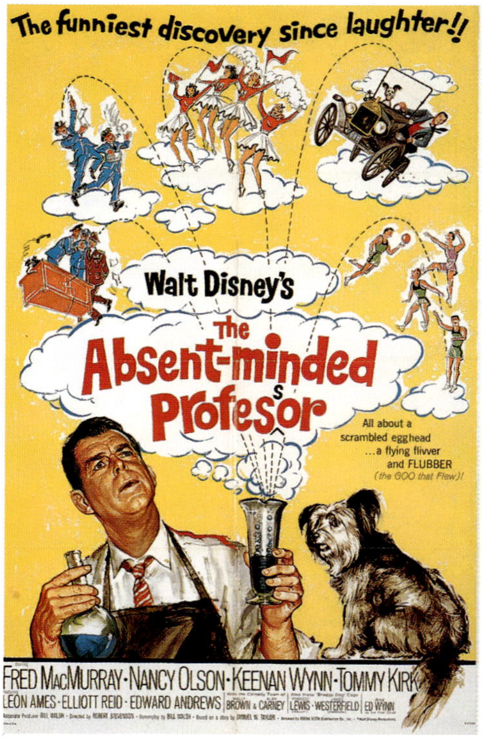

129. THE ABSENT-MINDED PROFESSOR, 1961

130. VILLAGE OF THE DAMNED, 1960

131. ROCKET ATTACK, U.S.A., 1961

132. BATTLE BEYOND THE SUN, 1962

133. KING KONG VS. GODZILLA, 1962

134. THE DAY MARS INVADED EARTH, 1962

135. 7 FACES OF DR. LAO, 1964

136. THE TIME TRAVELERS, 1964

137. FIRST MEN IN THE MOON, 1964

138. ROBINSON CRUSOE ON MARS, 1964

139. HERCULES AGAINST THE MOON MEN, 1964

140. SHE, 1965

141. OUR MAN FLINT, 1965

142. FANTASTIC VOYAGE, 1966

143. FAHRENHEIT 451, 1966, French poster

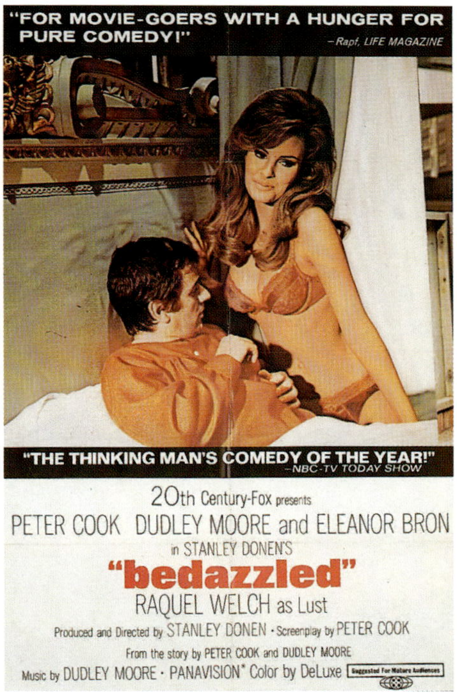

144. BEDAZZLED, 1967

145. CHITTY CHITTY BANG BANG, 1968

146. KING KONG ESCAPES, 1968

147. BARBARELLA, 1968, 1977 reissue

148. 2001: A SPACE ODYSSEY, 1968, 1974 reissue

149. ASTRO ZOMBIES, 1969

150. MISSION MARS, 1968

151. ON A CLEAR DAY YOU CAN SEE FOREVER, 1970

152. HOUSE OF DARK SHADOWS, 1970

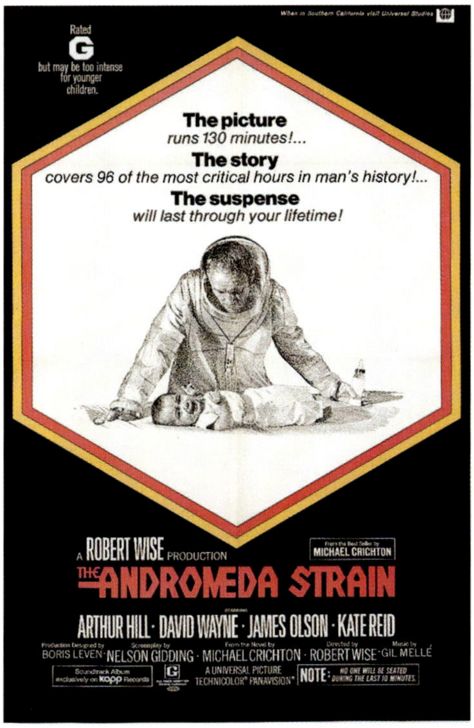

153. THE ANDROMEDA STRAIN, 1971

154. ESCAPE FROM THE PLANET OF THE APES, 1971

155. THE OMEGA MAN, 1971

156. PIGS (DADDY'S DEADLY DARLING), 1972

157. THE THING WITH TWO HEADS, 1972

158. CONQUEST OF THE PLANET OF THE APES, 1972

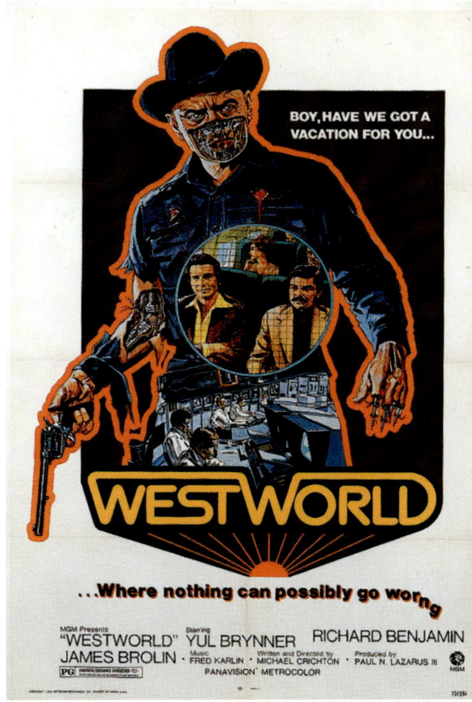

159. WESTWORLD, 1973

160. BATTLE FOR THE PLANET OF THE APES, 1973

161. SOYLENT GREEN, 1973

162. THE LITTLE PRINCE, 1974

163. LOGAN'S RUN, 1976, half-sheet

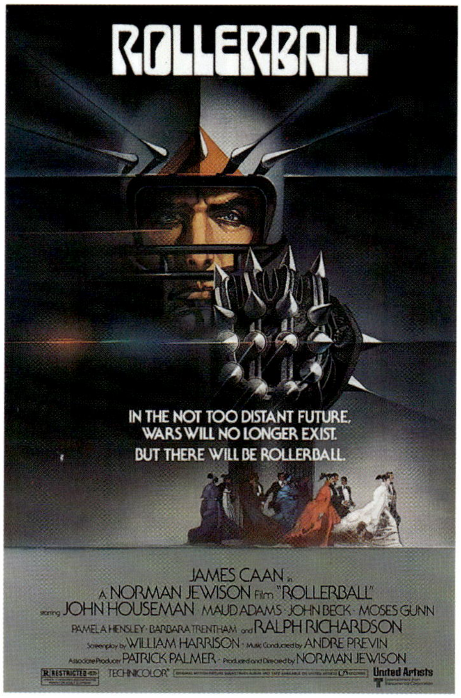

164. ROLLERBALL, 1975

165. INFRA-MAN, 1975

166. JABBERWOCKY, 1977

167. STAR WARS, 1977, half-sheet

168. STAR WARS, 1977, British quad

169. STAR WARS, 1977

170. STAR WARS, 1977

171. STAR WARS, 1977

172. STAR WARS CONCERT, 1978

173. THE EMPIRE STRIKES BACK, 1980,
three-sheet

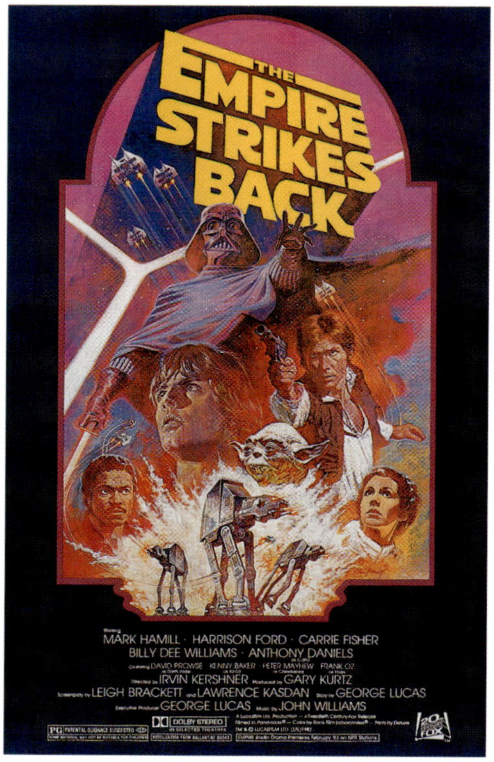

174. THE EMPIRE STRIKES BACK, 1980,
1982 reissue

175. THE EMPIRE STRIKES BACK, 1980,
special promotional poster

176. THE EMPIRE STRIKES BACK, 1980

177. THE EMPIRE STRIKES BACK, 1980

178. RETURN OF THE JEDI, 1983, British quad

179. RETURN OF THE JEDI, 1983

180. RETURN OF THE JEDI, 1983, insert

181. RETURN OF THE JEDI, 1983

182. STAR WARS, 1977, 1997 reissue

183. THE EMPIRE STRIKES BACK, 1980, 1997 reissue

184. RETURN OF THE JEDI, 1983, 1997 reissue

185. THE STAR WARS TRILOGY, 1997 reissue

186. THE PHANTOM MENACE, 1999

187. BUCK ROGERS, 1978

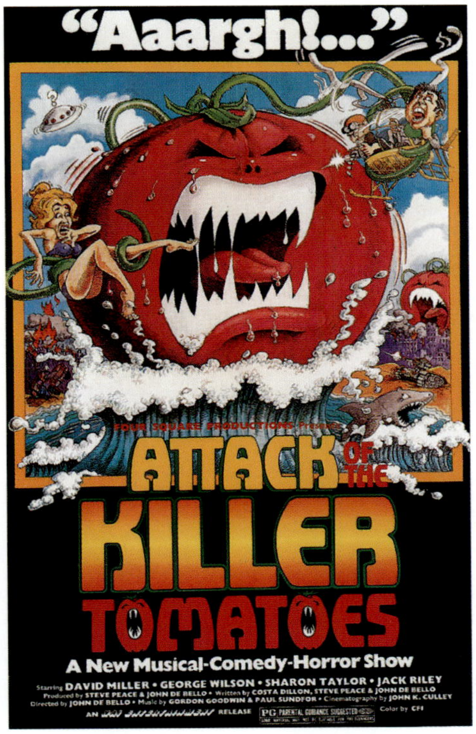

188. ATTACK OF THE KILLER TOMATOES, 1978

189. THE LORD OF THE RINGS, 1978

190. SUPERMAN, 1978

191. MAD MAX, 1979

192. STAR TREK: THE MOTION PICTURE, 1979

193. STAR TREK II: THE WRATH OF KHAN, 1982

194. STAR TREK II: THE WRATH OF KHAN, 1982

195. STAR TREK III: THE SEARCH FOR SPOCK, 1984

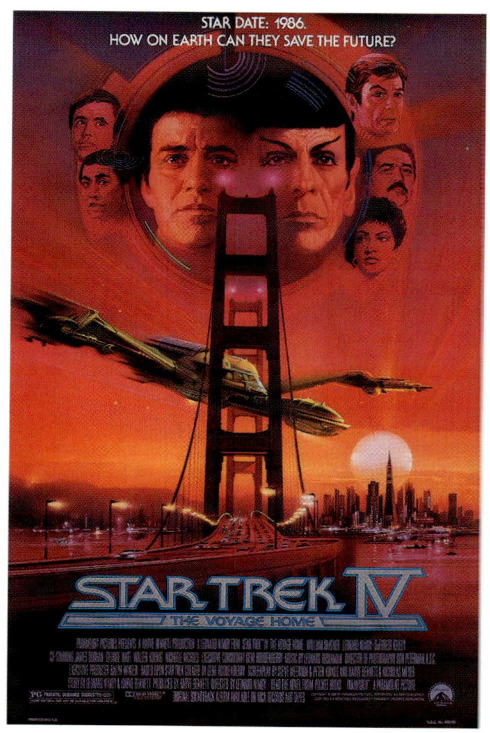

196. STAR TREK IV: THE VOYAGE HOME, 1986

197. STAR TREK V: THE FINAL FRONTIER, 1989

198. STAR TREK V: THE FINAL FRONTIER, 1989

199. STAR TREK VI: THE UNDISCOVERED COUNTRY, 1991

200. STAR TREK VI: THE UNDISCOVERED COUNTRY, 1991

201. STAR TREK: THE FACE OF THE FUTURE, 1991

202. STAR TREK GENERATIONS, 1994

203. STAR TREK GENERATIONS, 1994

204. STAR TREK FIRST CONTACT, 1996

205. STAR TREK FIRST CONTACT, 1996

206. STAR TREK INSURRECTION, 1998

207. ALIEN, 1979, special 1989 tenth anniversary poster

208. TIME AFTER TIME, 1979

209. THE WARRIORS, 1979

210. THE BLACK HOLE, 1979

211. GALAXINA, 1980

212. THE WATCHER IN THE WOODS, 1980

213. RAIDERS OF THE LOST ARK, 1981

214. HEAVY METAL, 1981

215. TIME BANDITS, 1981

216. EXCALIBUR, 1981

217. TRON, 1982

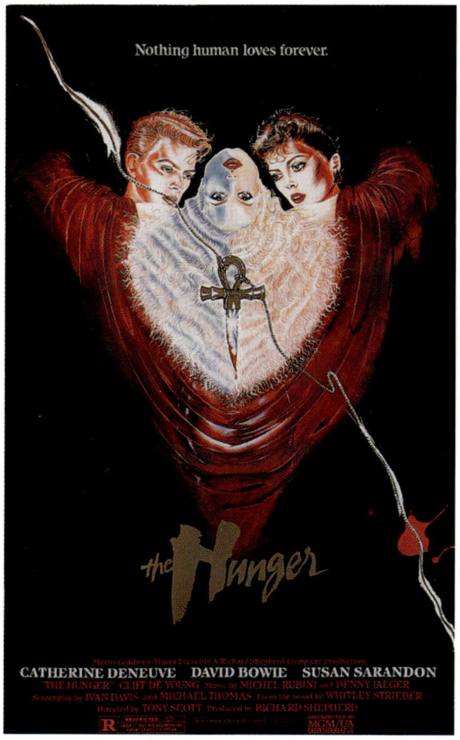

218. THE HUNGER, 1983

219. SOMETHING WICKED THIS WAY COMES, 1983

220. WAR GAMES, 1983

221. SUPERMAN III, 1983, Polish poster

222. INDIANA JONES AND THE TEMPLE OF DOOM, 1984

223. SUPERGIRL, 1984

224. THE ADVENTURES OF BUCKAROO BANZAI, 1984

225. ROMANCING THE STONE, 1984

226. RED SONJA, 1985

227. MAD MAX BEYOND THUNDERDOME, 1985

228. BACK TO THE FUTURE, 1985

229. WEIRD SCIENCE, 1985

230. LITTLE SHOP OF HORRORS, 1986

231. LABYRINTH, 1986

232. HOWARD THE DUCK, 1986

233. THE CLAN OF THE CAVE BEAR, 1986

234. ROBOCOP, 1987

235. NOT OF THIS EARTH, 1988

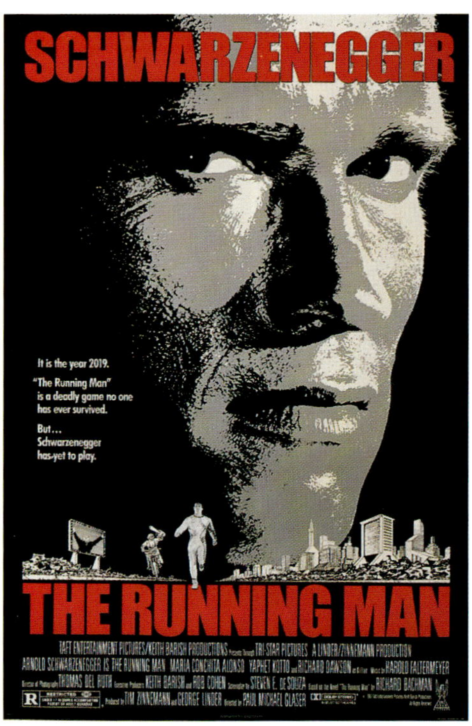

236. THE RUNNING MAN, 1987

237. RETURN OF THE KILLER TOMATOES, 1988

238. RETURN OF THE LIVING DEAD PART II, 1988

239. BACK TO THE FUTURE II, 1989

240. FIELD OF DREAMS, 1989

241. INDIANA JONES AND THE LAST CRUSADE, 1989

242. GHOSTBUSTERS II, 1989

243. BATMAN, 1989

244. BACK TO THE FUTURE III, 1990

245. GREMLINS 2, 1990

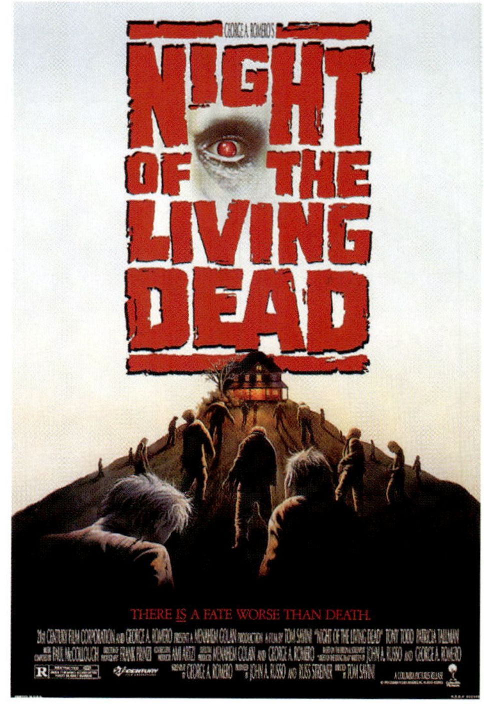

246. NIGHT OF THE LIVING DEAD, 1990

247. ROBOCOP 2, 1990

248. CHILD'S PLAY 2, 1990

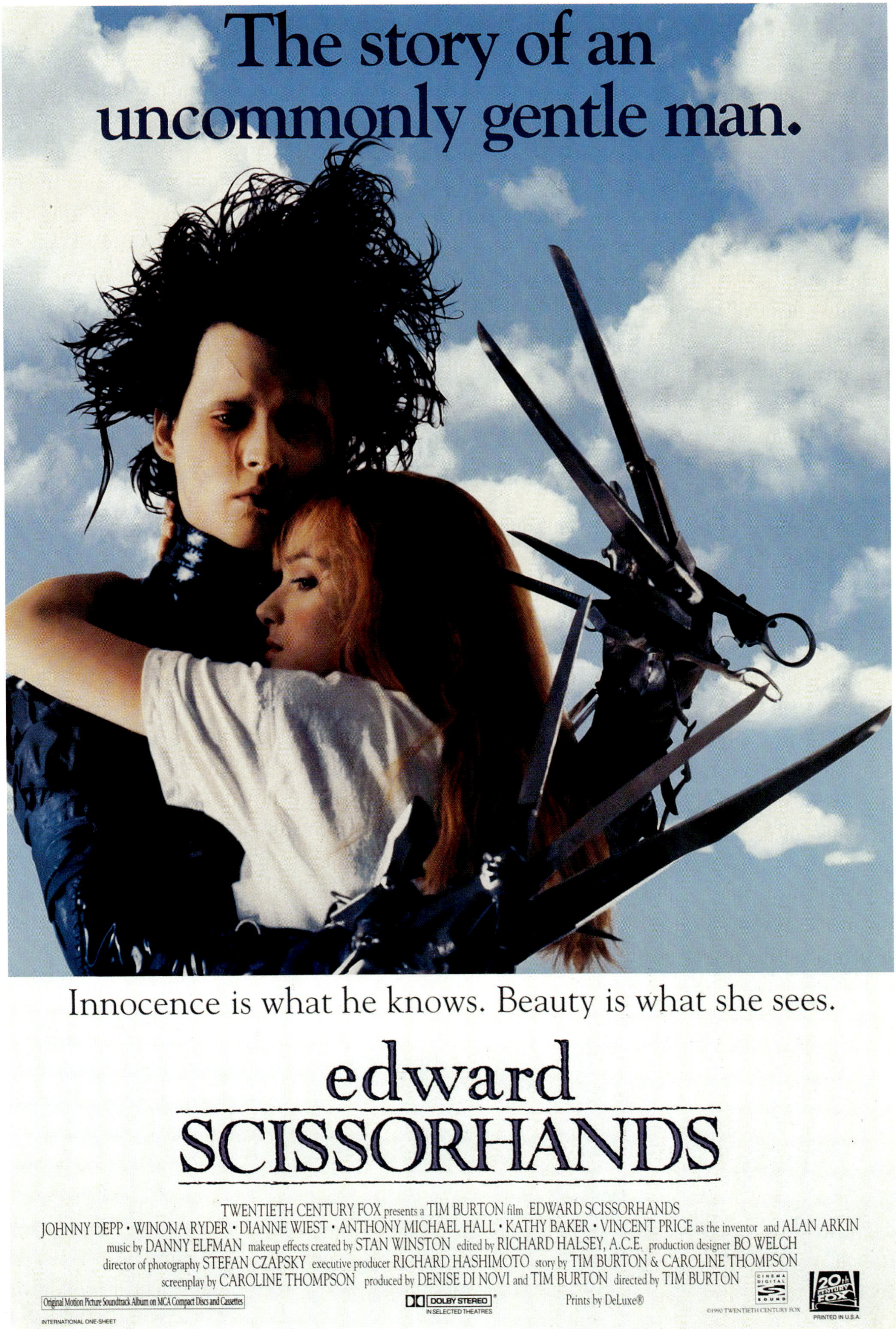

249. EDWARD SCISSORHANDS, 1990

250. THE ROCKETEER, 1991

251. SCANNERS II: THE NEW ORDER, 1991

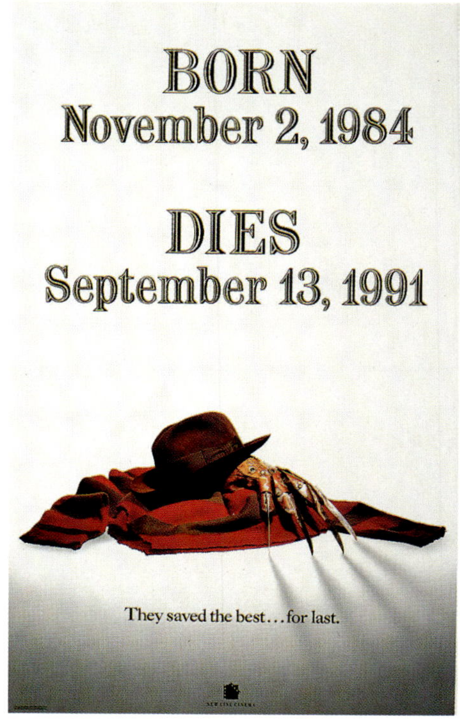

252. FREDDY'S DEAD: THE FINAL NIGHTMARE, 1991

253. BATMAN RETURNS, 1992

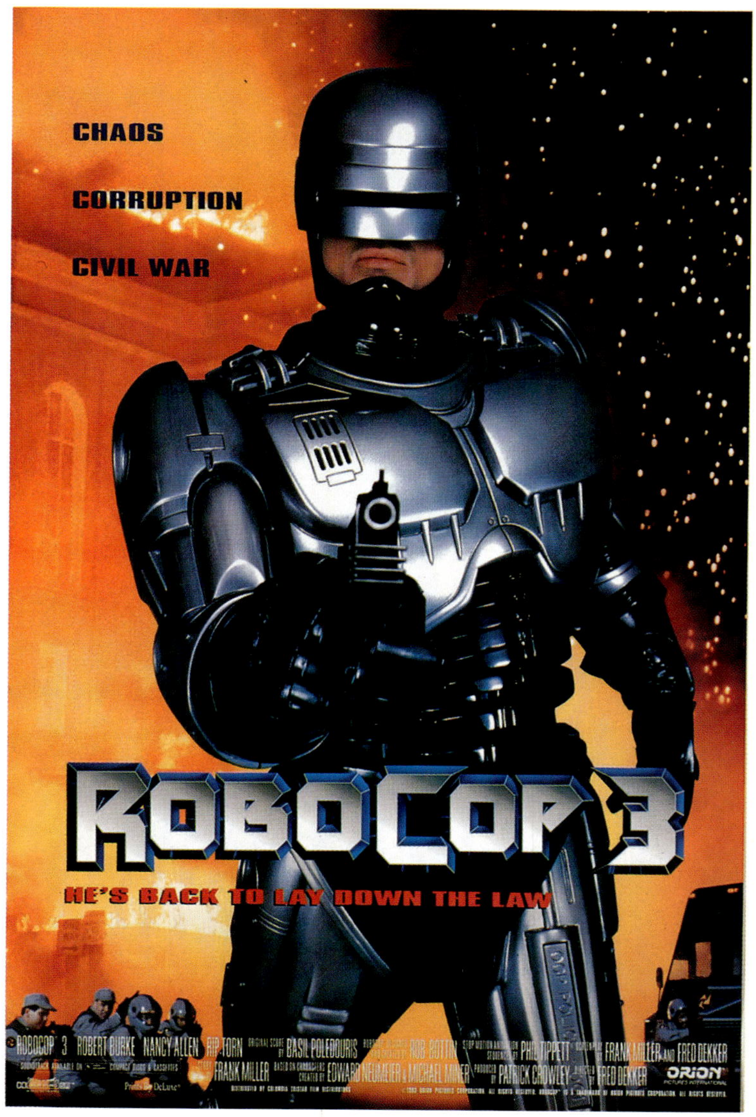

254. ROBOCOP 3, 1993

255. MIRACLE ON 34TH STREET, 1994

256. STARGATE, 1994

257. MIGHTY MORPHIN POWER RANGERS, 1995

258. WATERWORLD, 1995

259. BABE, 1995

260. BATMAN FOREVER, 1995

261. BATMAN FOREVER, 1995

262. BATMAN FOREVER, 1995

263. BATMAN FOREVER, 1995

264. BATMAN FOREVER, 1995

265. MARS ATTACKS, 1996

266. INDEPENDENCE DAY, 1996

267. THE DEVIL'S ADVOCATE, 1997

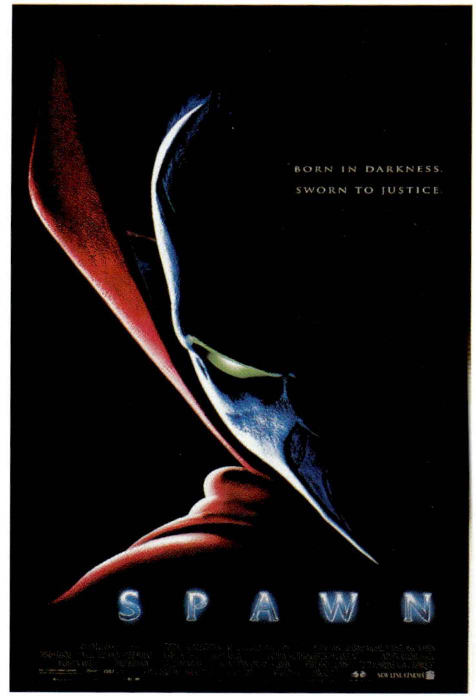

268. SPAWN, 1997

269. BATMAN & ROBIN, 1997

270. MEN IN BLACK, 1997

271. DEEP IMPACT, 1998

272. ARMAGEDDON, 1998

273. MEET JOE BLACK, 1998

274. GODZILLA, 1998

275. THE MUMMY, 1999

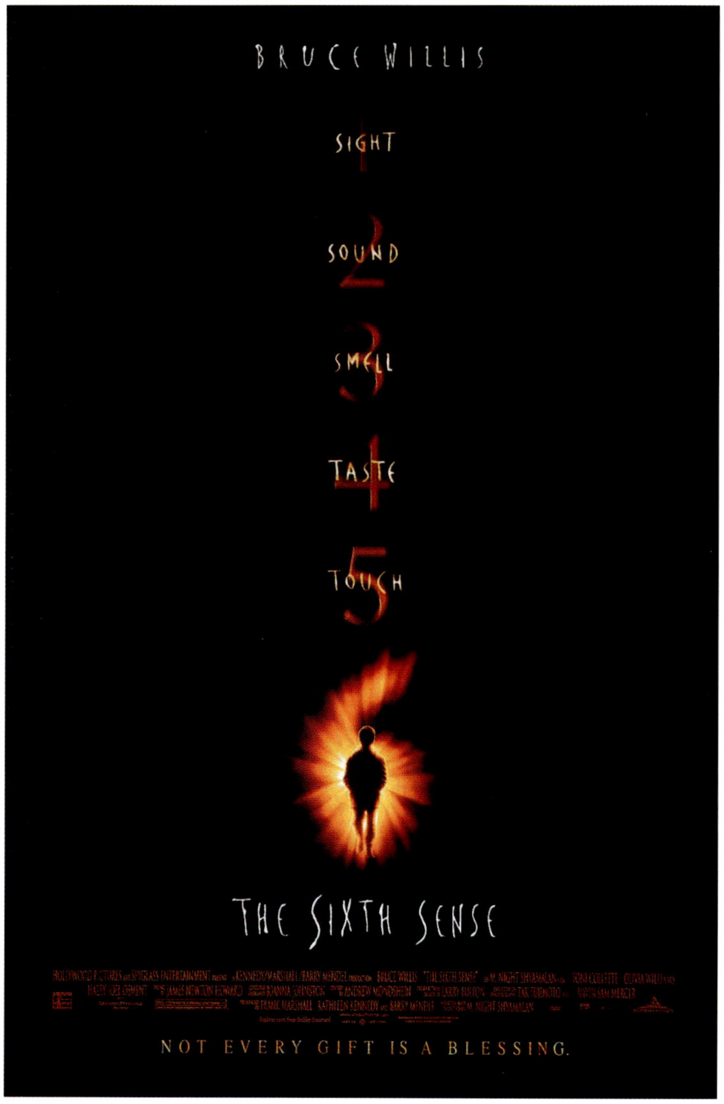

276. THE SIXTH SENSE, 1999

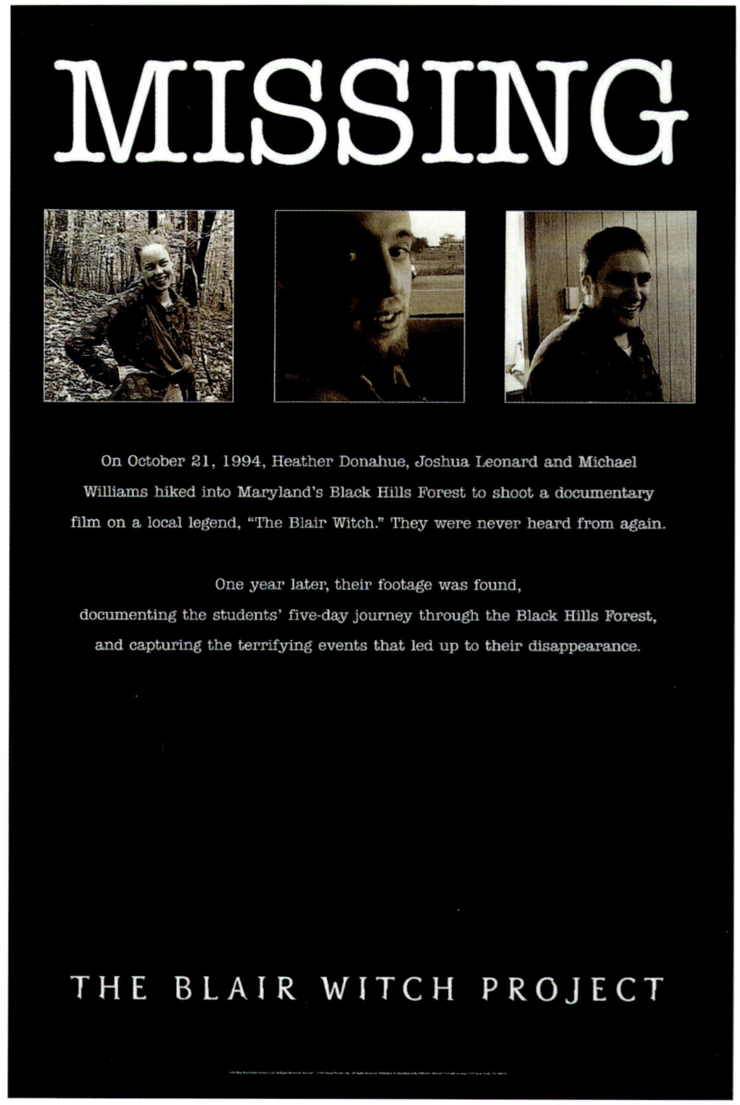

277. THE BLAIR WITCH PROJECT, 1999

278. THE MATRIX, 1999

279. END OF DAYS, 1999

280. SLEEPY HOLLOW, 1999

Horror Sci-Fi & Fantasy MOVIE POSTERS INDEX

Horror Sci-Fi & Fantasy MOVIE POSTERS INDEX